PROPERTY MANAGEMENT ACCOUNTING

A SURVIVAL GUIDE for NON-ACCOUNTANTS

PROPERTY MANAGEMENT ACCOUNTING:

A Survival Guide for Non-Accountants

Marc Levetin and Michael Monteiro

ISBN:1-4392-4161-9

This publication is designed to provide accurate and authoritative information in regard to the subject matter covered. It is offered with the understanding that the publisher is not engaged in rendering legal, accounting, or other professional services. If legal advice or other expert assistance is required, the services of a competent professional person should be sought.

Acknowledgements
Editorial Services: Nikki Van Noy (www.nikkivannoy.com)
Layout and Graphics: Andrea Diaz-Vaughn (www.diazvaughn.com)
Third-party Review: Dennis & Associates, P.C. (www.dennisassociates.com)

CONTENTS

Introduction

PROPERTY MANAGEMENT ACCOUNTING 101

IN THIS DAY and age, we're lucky to have software that takes care of the nuts and bolts of property management accounting. But even with software, you'll find it much easier to keep accurate records if you have an understanding of the basic accounting concepts upon which these programs are based. Buildium's *Property Management Accounting* is designed to teach you these concepts with property management specifically in mind.

Even the most complex property management accounting procedures can be broken down into a simple set of steps. Over the course of the coming pages we'll go over a variety of real world situations step-by-step, arming you with the information necessary to understand what your accounting software is doing behind the scenes. This guide will also help you understand how to read the three main financial statements (income statement, cash flow statement, and balance sheet) and provide some tips for keeping accurate financial records for the properties you manage.

One more thing ... you don't need an accounting degree or previous bookkeeping experience to keep accurate financial records. This guide will arm you with all the information you need. And if you *do* have an accounting background, you'll find some great refresher information in the following pages.

Practice Makes Perfect

The amount of information necessary to complete your accounting procedures will vary depending upon your job. For example, your accounting will obviously be more complex if you're a property manager overseeing dozens of properties as opposed to a landlord with just a few. With that in mind, we've organized this guide into different sections that will allow you to flip straight to the information you need.

Throughout this guide, practical examples will demonstrate basic accounting principles. These examples will give you the opportunity to record transactions ... just as you would in real life. We've made it easy for you to follow along by including a general journal with each example; you will record each transaction, and then check your answers in the next section. (For a complete explanation of general journals, turn to page 11.)

Chapter 1
ACCOUNTING CONCEPTS AND TERMINOLOGY

BEFORE LOOKING AT specific scenarios, let's start with some basics. Please note that this section is not meant to be a comprehensive guide, but rather a general overview of accounting procedures.

The Books

Before the days of accounting software, bookkeepers handwrote their company's financial transactions in enormous tomes (thus the very literal term, bookkeeper). As you can imagine, a bookkeeper's shelves were lined with large volumes, filled with column after column of handwritten records. From this paper-filled past, we get the term *the books*. Remember, each property you own is essentially its own company and will require the same bookkeeping measures as any other company.

As a property manager, it's your job to manage the books for your rental owners and homeowners' associations—even if you're working with software rather than real books. Each property, condominium, and association has its own set of books. When recording any financial transaction, it's important that you consider *where* it should be recorded. Always remember that a single transaction between two parties is actually recorded in two different sets of books; this can be especially confusing when the two parties are you and the rental owner. For example, when you collect management fees, the fees are recorded as an expense on the owner's books and as income on your books.

> **Each property, condominium and homeowners' association has its own set of books.**

Double-Entry Bookkeeping

Double-entry bookkeeping is at the very center of modern accounting. The primary rules of this system are simple:

1. For every transaction listed in the general journal (see page 11), there must be at least one debit and one credit.
2. The sum of all debits must equal the sum of all credits.

Don't worry if some of these concepts don't make sense right away ... they will become clear as we move further into this guide. We promise!

Chart of Accounts

At its simplest, an account is a category. Formally, an account is a summary of all debits and credits of a certain type for a company or property. A *chart of accounts* is a list of all accounts a landlord or property manager uses to categorize his transactions. The five major types of accounts are:

1. **Assets:** things a property owns
2. **Liabilities:** amounts a property owes
3. **Equity:** amounts that belong to the property's owners after subtracting what's owed
4. **Income:** amounts a property earns
5. **Expenses:** amounts a property spends

Flip to page 14 to see real examples of these accounts.

There are a couple of important things to keep in mind. First, while there are only five different *types* of accounts, you can have as many actual accounts as you want. It's entirely up to you and really just depends on your needs. For example, you can have a single account for tracking all utility expenses or you can have separate accounts for electricity, natural gas, water, and sewer.

Second, if you're working with a bookkeeper or an accounting firm, don't be shy about asking for advice. While there's no "right way" to set up your chart of accounts, there are a standard set of accounts most property managers will want to include—accounts for tracking things like rental income and management fees, for example.

Finally, when it comes to naming accounts, everyone seems to have an opinion. Some people like to give their accounts descriptive names; others prefer to use numbers. And still others insist that using both is the only way to go. Whatever your preference, be sure your software can accommodate it.

General Journal

The *general journal* (or book of original entry) is a chronological list of each and every financial transaction that occurs during the course of business. These transactions are called *general journal entries*. When you record a journal entry, you must have at least one debit and one credit *and* your debits and credits must balance out. In other words, the sum of all debits must equal the sum of all credits for a single transaction.

> **Each transaction in the general journal must balance out—this means that your total debits must equal total credits.**

Here's an outline of a general journal entry:

TRANS. NO.	DATE	ACCOUNT NAMES AND EXPLANATION	DEBIT	CREDIT
		Name of account being debited	Amount	
		Name of account being credited		Amount
		Optional: short description		

And here are a few examples:

TRANS. NO.	DATE	ACCOUNT NAMES AND EXPLANATION	DEBIT	CREDIT
1	Jan. 1	Checking Account	1,000	
		Rent Income		1,000
		Rent payment from Sam Paul		

TRANS. NO.	DATE	ACCOUNT NAMES AND EXPLANATION	DEBIT	CREDIT
150	June 5	Checking Account	1,050	
		Rent Income		1,000
		Late Fee Income		50
		Rent payment from Sam Paul		

By the end of the year, your general journal will probably have hundreds of entries just like these.

When it comes to double-entry bookkeeping, remember that each transaction in the general journal must have *at least* one debit and *at least* one credit. That doesn't mean you need an equal number of debits and credits. For example, you may have a journal entry with one debit and two credits—that's okay as long as the total *amount* of all the debits equals the total of all the credits.

General Ledger

The *general ledger* is a compilation of individual accounts, also called *T accounts* because they are shaped like the letter T.

Here are the T accounts for the general journal entries we made above.

CHECKING ACCOUNT				RENT INCOME				LATE FEE INCOME		
TRANS. NO.	DEBIT	CREDIT		TRANS. NO.	DEBIT	CREDIT		TRANS. NO.	DEBIT	CREDIT
1	1,000			1		1,000		—	—	—
—	—	—		—	—	—		150		50
150	1,050			150		1,000				

Relating the General Journal to the General Ledger

The general journal and the general ledger are really two different views of the same information. The general journal shows transactions in chronological order, while the general ledger shows transaction totals by account.

So why do you need both? Think of the general journal as a diary of all the transactions that affect your property. Though the journal is a great way of seeing what happened when, it's not so good for summarizing information. For example, while it can tell you how much you spent for supplies on a particular purchase, it can't tell you how much you've spent for supplies across all purchases. That's where the general ledger comes in.

Debit and Credit Accounts

As we've already discussed, each transaction has at least one debit and one credit. You'll also recall that each individual transaction must balance to zero—that is, the sum of the debits must equal the sum of the credits.

But how do you know when to debit and when to credit a particular account? You start by knowing whether the account is a *debit* account or *credit* account. Once you know this, the rest is easy.

- Debits *increase* the value of *debit* accounts.
- Credits *increase* the value of *credit* accounts.

> **TIP>>**
> Having a hard time keeping all of this straight? Just remember, assets and expenses are debit accounts. Everything else is a credit account.

If you're working with a debit account *and* if you want to *increase* its value, you debit it. If you want to *decrease* its value, you credit it. The opposite is true for credit accounts. The rule is easy—the trickier part is figuring out what kind of account you're dealing with. For that, you'll just have to commit the following to memory:

- Assets and expenses are *debit* accounts; debits *increase* the value of debit accounts.
- Income, equity, and liabilities are *credit* accounts; credits *increase* the value of credit accounts.

Here's a handy chart to help you remember all of this. Be sure to read the chart from the outside in. For example, debits increase the value of an asset account, while credits decrease them.

DEBITS	ACCOUNT TYPE	CREDITS
	Assets *(things a property owns)*	
Increase	Bank Accounts • Prepaid Expenses Accounts Receivable • Property and Equipment Other Amounts Due to the Company Accumulated Depreciation	Decrease
	Liabilities *(amounts a property owes)*	
Decrease	Security Deposits • Prepaid Rent Accounts Payable • Pet Deposits Credit Cards • Loans	Increase
	Equity *(amounts that belong to the property's owners after subtracting what's owed)*	
Decrease	Owner Equity	Increase
	Income *(amounts a property earns)*	
Decrease	Rent Income • Late Fee Income Utility Income • Laundry Income Repairs Income	Increase
	Expenses *(amounts a property spends)*	
Increase	Management Fees • Repairs Supplies • Insurance • Utilities Advertizing • Depreciation Expenses Interest	Decrease

Accrual versus Cash Accounting

The last concept to consider is *when* to record a transaction on your property's books. The answer depends on which accounting method you choose: *cash* or *accrual*. **With the *cash method of accounting,* you record income and expenses only when money changes hands.** You record income when your tenants pay you and you record expenses when you pay your vendors.

With the *accrual method,* you record income and expenses the moment you earn money or owe it, regardless of when the money actually changes hands. So which method should you use? The answer is: It's up to you. While the vast majority of property managers keep their books on a cash basis for the sake of simplicity, some choose accrual accounting because they believe it provides a more accurate picture of how a property is doing.

You can choose different accounting methods for your company and each of the properties you manage, but the IRS requires that you receive their approval before changing your method once your initial choice has been made. If you're not sure which method is right for you, consult your accountant.

Cash Accounting

With cash accounting, you record the income on January 5 when Sam Paul
pays his rent.

TRANS. NO.	DATE	ACCOUNT NAMES AND EXPLANATION	DEBIT	CREDIT
1	Jan. 5	Checking Account	1,000	
		Rent Income		1,000
		Rent payment from Sam Paul		

ACCRUAL Accounting

With accrual accounting, you record the income on January 1 when Sam Paul's
rent is *due*.

TRANS. NO.	DATE	ACCOUNT NAMES AND EXPLANATION	DEBIT	CREDIT
1	Jan. 1	Accounts Receivable	1,000	
		Rent Income		1,000
		January rent due from Sam Paul		

Cash Accounting

When you're on a cash basis, you record the expense on January 4 when you *pay* the bill.

TRANS. NO.	DATE	ACCOUNT NAMES AND EXPLANATION	DEBIT	CREDIT
1	Jan. 4	Utility Expense	100	
		Checking Account		100
		Payment to electric company		

ACCRUAL Accounting

When you're on an accrual basis, you record the expense on January 1 when you *receive* the bill.

TRANS. NO.	DATE	ACCOUNT NAMES AND EXPLANATION	DEBIT	CREDIT
1	Jan. 1	Utility Expense	100	
		Accounts Payable		100
		Bill from electric company		

Financial Statements

Now that we've covered basic accounting terminology and concepts, it's time to take a look at the three main financial statements: the income statement, cash flow statement, and balance sheet.

Income Statement

An *income statement* (also called a *profit and loss statement* or *P&L*) is a summary of a property's profit or loss during a given period of time. It shows total income, expenses, and net income—the amount of income that remains after subtracting expenses.

The purpose of the income statement is to show whether a property made or lost money during the specified period. The important thing to remember is that it represents a period of time.

Cash Flow Statement

While an income statement tells you whether a property made a profit, a *cash flow statement* tells you whether it generated cash. Like the income statement, the cash flow statement represents a specific period of time.

It's important to note that if you use accrual accounting, your property's net income may not equal the amount of cash it generated for the period. That's because with accrual accounting, you recognize income and expenses the moment you earn money or owe it, regardless of when money changes hands. As a result, a property that's turning a profit in the eyes of the IRS may actually end up with less cash than when it started. That's why the cash flow statement is important; it helps you see if a property has enough cash to pay its bills.

1 MAIN STREET
INCOME STATEMENT
Jan. 1 – Jan. 31

Income	
Rent Income	1,100
Late Fee Income	100
Total Income	**1,200**
Expenses	
Repairs	200
Management Fees	200
Total Expenses	**400**
Net Income	**800**

1 MAIN STREET
CASH FLOW STATEMENT
Jan. 1 – Jan. 31

Net Income	**800**
Accounts Receivable	-300
Accounts Payable	200
Net cash increase for period	**700**
Cash at beginning of period	0
Cash at end of period	**700**

Balance Sheet

A *balance sheet* shows what a company owns and what it owes at a **specific point in time**. It's important to note that while income and cash flow statements show an overview over a *period* of time, balance sheets show a snapshot of a specific *point* in time.

A balance sheet is divided into three parts: assets, liabilities, and equity. Remember assets are things a company owns, liabilities are amounts a company owes, and equity is what belongs to the company's owners after subtracting what's owed.

1 MAIN STREET
BALANCE SHEET
(as of Jan. 31)

Assets		Liabilities	
Rent Bank Account	1,700	Security Deposit Liability	1,000
Deposit Bank Account	2,000	Prepaid Rent Liability	1,000
Accounts Receivable	300	Accounts Payable	200
		Total Liabilities	**2,200**
		Equity	
		Net Income	800
		Retained Earnings	1,000
		Total Equity	**1,800**
Total Assets	**4000**	**Total Liabilities and Equity**	**4,000**

Retained earnings: net profits or losses from prior years that have been not been distributed to the company's owners

Net income: year-to-date profits or losses

Relating the Main Financial Statements

Although each financial statement is different, keep in mind that they're all related. For example, a company's assets and equity increase (or decrease) when a company makes a profit (or loss). While no one financial statement provides the whole picture, together they provide the information necessary to determine how a company or property is doing.

**1 MAIN STREET
BALANCE SHEET**
(as of Jan. 31)

Assets		Liabilities	
Rent Bank Account	1,700	Security Deposit Liability	1,000
Deposit Bank Account	2,000	Prepaid Rent Liability	1,000
Accounts Receivable	300	Accounts Payable	200
		Total Liabilities	**2,200**
		Equity	
		Net Income	800
		Retained Earnings	1,000
		Total Equity	**1,800**
Total Assets	**4,000**	**Total Liabilities and Equity**	**4,000**

1 MAIN STREET
CASH FLOW STATEMENT
Jan. 1 – Jan. 31

Net Income	800
Accounts Receivable	-300
Accounts Payable	200
Net cash increase for period	700
Cash at beginning of period	0
Cash at end of period	700

1 MAIN STREET
INCOME STATEMENT
Jan. 1 – Jan. 31

Income	
Rent Income	1,100
Late Fee Income	100
Total Income	1,200
Expenses	
Repairs	200
Management Fees	200
Total Expenses	400
Net Income	800

TRANSACTION TAKES PLACE

THE ACCOUNTING CYCLE

RECORD (OR "JOURNALIZE") TRANSACTION
in the general journal

POST ENTRIES
to the general ledger

PREPARE FINANCIAL STATEMENTS

Putting it all together: The Accounting Cycle

We've already discussed a number of accounting concepts, including the chart of accounts, journal entries, and general ledger. But how do they fit together and how are they used in the real world? The answer is the *accounting cycle.*

It sounds complicated, but the accounting cycle is nothing more than a series of steps for recording business transactions from the time they take place to the time they appear in financial statements. The chart of accounts, general journal, and general ledger are the tools you'll use along the way to complete these steps:

1. The transaction takes place (for example, you collect rent, pay a bill, or refund a tenant's security deposit).

2. You *journalize* or record the transaction in the general journal in chronological order.

3. You *post* the entries to the appropriate T accounts on the general ledger.

4. You total your accounts and use those totals to prepare your financial statements.

CHAPTER 2
LANDLORD ACCOUNTING

IF YOU'RE LIKE most landlords, your job requires a lot of juggling. You have to take care of your property and your tenants, simultaneously making sure that your investment is well cared for and that your tenants are happy. These two things, in and of themselves, can easily be a full-time job.

No matter how good you are at managing your property and caring for your tenants, though, the bottom line is that no landlord can run a successful, profitable business without consistently adhering to basic accounting procedures. When you think about it, your two main tasks—taking care of your property and taking care of your tenants—inherently involve cash flow. You're probably frequently spending money on property upkeep and, meanwhile, receiving rent money from tenants on a monthly basis. And this is not to mention all the other miscellaneous expenditures that likely occur on a weekly basis.

So the bottom line is, accounting *is* an important aspect of any landlord's job. In this chapter we'll go over the accounting procedures that you, as a landlord, are most likely to deal with on a regular basis. Many of these concepts are most easily understood when they're set in real world scenarios. So for our purposes, let's assume you're the proud new owner of a two-unit property called the Arlington. You have a few minor repairs to make and are anxious to get your first tenants settled in.

Let's get started.

Setting Up the Books

It may sound silly, but the first question you'll need to ask yourself is: **Exactly whose books am I keeping?** It's not necessarily intuitive, but even as a landlord (as opposed to a property manager overseeing multiple properties) you're handling two different sets of books—one for your personal finances and another specifically for the Arlington.

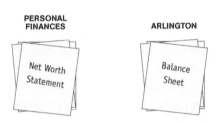

So why is it important to separate your rental properties from your personal finances? For starters, you'll need to report rental property income and expenses separately on your tax return. But, more importantly, it's hard to gauge how your properties are performing without keeping a separate set of books for each one.

Contributing Funds

Now that you've separated your property's books from your own, it's time to figure out how much money you'll need to get your property up and running. You decide to deposit $10,000 in a separate bank account set up specifically for the Arlington; this money will cover the property's expenses until the rent starts rolling in. We'll call this the Arlington's *operating bank account*.

Your next step is to figure out how to record the $10,000 deposit on the Arlington's books. You've already learned that every transaction requires at least one debit and one credit. But which accounts do you debit and which do you credit? Let's review what we know so far:

- You deposited $10,000 in the Arlington's operating bank account to cover start-up costs.
- The operating bank account is an asset (see the chart on page 14 for a review).
- Assets are **debit** accounts; debits **increase** the value of debit accounts.
- The deposit **increased** (debited) the bank balance.
- You need to **credit** another account to offset this debit.

NOTE>>

When we refer to *equity*, **we're not talking about the difference between the property's fair market value and the unpaid mortgage balance. Instead, we're talking about the difference between the property's assets (what it owns) and its liabilities (what it owes).**

But which account do you credit? An equity account called *owner contributions*. Remember that *equity* is the amount that belongs to the property's owners after subtracting what's owed. In this case, nothing is owed, so the total equity is $10,000.

TRANS. NO.	DATE		DEBIT	CREDIT
1	Dec. 1	Operating Bank Account		
		Owner Contributions		
		Initial capital investment for the Arlington		

Paying Bills

As things stand, the Arlington is a good property. And after a bit of work, it will be a *great* property—one that commands the best tenants and the highest rent in the area. With your eye on the prize, you decide to have the apartments painted and the hardwood floors refinished.

You call a few folks and finally settle on Do-It-All General Contracting. They give you an estimate of $6,000 and ask for a $2,000 check up front to cover the cost of the paint and materials.

First, you need to record the check to Do-It-All General Contracting on the books. Again, let's review what we know:

- You wrote a $2,000 check for maintenance from the Arlington's operating bank account.
- The bank account is an asset and maintenance is an expense.
- Assets and expenses are **debit** accounts; debits **increase** the value of debit accounts.
- The check **decreased** (credited) the bank balance and **increased** (debited) maintenance expense.

CASH VERSUS ACCRUAL ACCOUNTING>>

Remember, with cash accounting you record expenses when you pay bills, not when you receive them (for a refresher on cash and accrual accounting, see page 15). Since the vast majority of rental owners use cash accounting, for the remainder of this guide we'll assume you are keeping the books on a cash basis. When applicable, special sections follow showing how things look on an accrual basis; if you are not using accrual accounting, feel free to skip over these sections.

TRANS. NO.	DATE		DEBIT	CREDIT
1	Dec. 1	Operating Bank Account	10,000	
		Owner Contributions		10,000
		Initial capital investment for the Arlington		
2	Dec. 5	**Maintenance Expense**		
		Operating Bank Account		
		Payment to Do-It-All General Contracting		

TIP>>
If you use a credit card instead of a check for purchases, you'll need to record the purchases differently; we'll go over that on page 32.

ACCRUAL Paying Bills

Cash accounting readers can skip this section.

With cash accounting, you recorded the maintenance expense when you wrote the $2,000 check to Do-It-All General Contracting. With accrual accounting, you record the expense when you receive the bill—in other words, *before* you pay it. Here is what we know:

- You owe Do-It-All General Contracting $2,000 for maintenance.
- Maintenance is an expense.
- Expenses are *debit* accounts; debits *increase* the value of debit accounts.
- You need to *credit* another account to offset the debit.

With accrual accounting, you record an expense when you receive the bill, even if you have not yet paid it.

So which account do you credit? The answer is a special liability account called *accounts payable*; this account represents money your property owes to vendors. Liability accounts are credit accounts, so you record the bill by debiting maintenance and crediting accounts payable.

TRANS. NO.	DATE		DEBIT	CREDIT
2	Dec. 5	Maintenance Expense	2,000	
		Accounts Payable		2,000
		Bill from Do-It-All General Contracting		

Notice that you haven't paid the bill yet; you've just recorded the expense. You want Do-It-All General Contracting to get started right away so you decide to write them a check.

Here is what we know:

- You are writing a $2,000 check from the Arlington's bank account to pay money owed to Do-It-All General Contracting.
- The bank account is an asset and accounts payable is a liability.
- Assets are *debit* accounts; debits *increase* the value of debit accounts.
- Liabilities are *credit* accounts; credits *increase* the value of credit accounts.
- The check will *decrease* the bank balance and *decrease* accounts payable.

TRANS. NO.	DATE		DEBIT	CREDIT
3	Dec. 5	Accounts Payable	2,000	
		Operating Bank Account		2,000
		Payment to Do-It-All General Contracting		

Making Purchases by Credit Card

In order to rent your units as soon as possible, you decide to run an ad in the local newspaper. The ad costs $75, which you put on your business credit card.

Before you record the credit card purchase, let's review what we know:

- You put the $75 advertising fee on your credit card.
- Advertising is an expense and your credit card is a liability (because you owe the credit card company money for purchases you make).
- Expenses are *debit* accounts; debits *increase* the value of debit accounts.
- Liabilities are *credit* accounts; credits *increase* the value of credit accounts.
- The purchase *increased* (debited) advertising expense and *increased* (credited) your credit card liability.

TRANS. NO.	DATE		DEBIT	CREDIT
2	Dec. 5	Maintenance Expense	2,000	
		Operating Bank Account		2,000
		Payment to Do-It-All General Contracting		
3	Dec. 6	**Advertising Expense**		
		Business Credit Card		
		Payment to local newspaper		

Collecting Rent and Security Deposits

Your ad works. You get a number of responses and after running credit and background checks, you accept your first applicant, Sam Paul.

Let's look at Sam's lease:

UNIT	TENANT	LEASE START	LEASE TERM	MONTHLY RENT	SECURITY DEPOSIT
1	Sam Paul	Jan. 1	1 year	$1,000	$1,000

In order to secure his lease, Sam Paul writes a check for $2,000 to cover both rent and his security deposit. You promptly deposit your first tenant check into the Arlington's bank account.

Now record the deposit on the books. Again, let's review what we know:

- You deposited Sam Paul's $2,000 check into the Arlington's bank account.
- Of that total amount, $1,000 is for first month's rent and $1,000 is for security.
- The bank account is an asset, rent is income, and Sam's security deposit is a liability (because the security deposit still belongs to Sam).
- Assets are *debit* accounts; debits *increase* the value of debit accounts.
- Income and liability accounts are *credit* accounts; credits *increase* the value of credit accounts.
- The deposit *increased* (debited) the bank balance, *increased* (credited) rent income, and *increased* (credited) security deposit liability.

YOUR TURN

Go ahead and record the deposit in the Arlington's general journal and general ledger.

TRANS. NO.	DATE		DEBIT	CREDIT
3	Dec. 6	Advertising Expense	75	
		Business Credit Card		75
		Payment to local newspaper		
4	**Dec. 22**	**Operating Bank Account**		
		Rent Income		
		Security Deposit Liability		
		Security deposit and first month's rent payment from Sam Paul		

`ACCRUAL` Collecting Rent and Security Deposits

Cash accounting readers can skip this section.

Once again, remember that with accrual accounting, you record income and expenses as you earn or owe money, regardless of when money actually changes hands. This means you record the first month's rent and security deposit the moment they are due, even if you haven't actually received payment yet.

Here's what we know:

- Sam Paul owes $1,000 for his first month's rent and $1,000 for the security deposit.
- Rent is income and the security deposit is a liability.
- Income and liability accounts are *credit* accounts; credits *increase* the value of credit accounts.
- You need to *debit* another account to offset the credit.

So which account do you debit? A special asset account called *accounts receivable;* this account represents money other people (like tenants) owe the property.

TRANS. NO.	DATE		DEBIT	CREDIT
5	Dec. 22	Accounts Receivable	2,000	
		Rent Income		1,000
		Security Deposit Liability		1,000
		Security deposit and first month's rent due from Sam Paul		

It's important to note that you now have $1,000 of rent income and $1,000 security deposit liability on the books even though you haven't yet collected any money. Here's what happens when you *do* collect the money and make the deposit.

TRANS. NO.	DATE		DEBIT	CREDIT
6	Dec. 22	Operating Bank Account	2,000	
		Accounts Receivable		2,000
		Security deposit and first month's rent payment from Sam Paul		

Holding Security Deposits

Soon after depositing Sam Paul's check, it occurs to you that the money for his security deposit is sitting in your operating account. Your books show that this money doesn't belong to you, but leaving it in the operating account seems like a good way to accidentally spend money that isn't yours. You wisely decide it's best to keep all of your tenants' security deposits in a separate bank account where the funds cannot be inadvertently spent.

This means it's time for you to open a new bank account. Remember, you've already deposited Sam Paul's security deposit money into your operating account so you'll need to transfer it to your new security deposit holding account.

> **TIP>>**
> When you hold security deposits, you have both an asset *and* a liability on the books.

YOUR TURN

Go ahead and record the transfer in the Arlington's general journal and general ledger.

TRANS. NO.	DATE		DEBIT	CREDIT
4	Dec. 22	Operating Bank Account	2,000	
		Rent Income		1,000
		Security Deposit Liability		1,000
		Security deposit and first month's rent payment from Sam Paul		
5	Dec. 22	**Security Deposit Bank Account**		
		Operating Bank Account		
		Security deposit transfer to security deposit account		

Discounting Rent

After a few uneventful months, Sam Paul calls to let you know there are some broken steps on the Arlington's front porch. He reminds you that he does carpentry for a living and offers to repair the steps for $200. Rather than paying him cash, you agree to take $200 off next month's rent. Sam then writes you a check for the balance, which you deposit into the Arlington's bank account.

Here is what we know:

- You deducted $200 from Sam's rent.
- You deposited Sam's $800 rent check into the Arlington's bank account; an asset.
- Assets are *debit* accounts; debits *increase* the value of debit accounts.
- Income accounts are *credit* accounts; credits *increase* the value of credit accounts.

You know how to record the $800 deposit, but what about the $200 you deducted from Sam's rent? The answer is you *debit* repairs and *credit* rent income, but why? When you deduct money from Sam's rent, it's as if you are giving him $200 to repair the steps (an expense), which he then gives back to you as rent (income).

YOUR TURN

Go ahead and record the $200 discount and $800 deposit in the Arlington's general journal and general ledger.

TRANS. NO.	DATE		DEBIT	CREDIT
5	Dec. 22	Security Deposit Bank Account	1,000	
		Operating Bank Account		1,000
		Security deposit transfer to security deposit account		
6	Apr. 28	**Repairs Expense**		
		Rent Income		
		Rent adjustment for repairs by Sam Paul		
7	May 1	**Operating Bank Account**		
		Rent Income		
		Rent payment from Sam Paul		

ACCRUAL Discounting Rent

Cash accounting readers can skip this section.

Here's how the same transaction looks on an accrual basis:

TRANS. NO.	DATE		DEBIT	CREDIT
8	Apr. 28	Repairs Expense	200	
		Accounts Receivable		200
		Rent adjustment for repairs by Sam Paul		
9	May 1	Accounts Receivable	1,000	
		Rent Income		1,000
		Rent due from Sam Paul		
10	May 1	Operating Bank Account	800	
		Accounts Receivable		800
		Rent payment from Sam Paul		

Let's look at the three transactions in this series. The $200 debit to repairs makes sense, but why is the credit issued to accounts receivable rather than accounts payable? After all, you owe Sam $200 for fixing the steps. In this particular scenario, because Sam owes you $1,000, you reduce accounts receivable (what he owes you) by $200 instead of adding the same amount to accounts payable.

Next you debit (increase) accounts receivable by $1,000 because Sam still owes $1,000 in rent as usual. The final transaction is Sam's $800 rent payment deposited to the Arlington's bank account.

Withholding Security Deposits

Thirty days before his lease expires, Sam provides written notice that he will not be renewing his lease. After he moves out, you do a walk-through of the unit and discover that Sam caused some damage while loading his moving van. Several walls are damaged, along with the front door. You're not sure exactly what happened but it's clear this damage goes beyond "normal wear and tear." Do-It-All General Contracting estimates it will cost $500 to fix the damage, which you decide to withhold from Sam's security deposit.

You know how to record an expense, but what happens when you withhold a portion of Sam's security deposit? Remember when you *hold* security, you have a liability on the books because you're holding someone else's money. When you *withhold* security, you reduce the liability *and* recognize income equal to the amount withheld. We'll call this *other income* so we can track it separately from rent income.

Here is what we know:

- You withheld $500 from Sam's security deposit.
- Liability and income accounts are *credit* accounts; credits *increase* the value of credit accounts.
- You need to *decrease* (debit) security deposit liability and *increase* (credit) other income by $500.

YOUR TURN

Go ahead and record the withheld security deposit in the Arlington's general journal and general ledger.

TRANS. NO.	DATE		DEBIT	CREDIT
6	Apr. 28	Repairs Expense	200	
		Rent Income		200
		Rent adjustment for repairs by Sam Paul		
7	May 1	Operating Bank Account	800	
		Rent Income		800
		Rent payment from Sam Paul		
8	Jan. 4	**Security Deposit Liability**		
		Other Income		
		Security deposit withheld for damage		

Now it's time to pay Do-It-All. Remember, you just withheld $500 from Sam's security deposit to pay for the repairs. You *could* write a check from the security deposit bank account but you decide to transfer $500 to your operating account and write the check from there.

YOUR TURN

Go ahead and record the transaction in the Arlington's general journal and general ledger.

TRANS. NO.	DATE		DEBIT	CREDIT
8	Jan. 4	Security Deposit Liability	500	
		Other Income		500
		Security deposit withheld for damage		
9	Jan. 4	**Operating Bank Account**		
		Security Deposit Bank Account		
		Security deposit transfer to operating account		
10	Jan. 5	**Repairs Expense**		
		Operating Bank Account		
		Payment to Do-It-All General Contracting		

ACCRUAL Withholding Security Deposits

Cash accounting readers can skip this section.

Here's how things look when withholding security on an accrual basis:

TRANS. NO.	DATE		DEBIT	CREDIT
11	Jan. 4	Accounts Receivable	500	
		Other Income		500
		Damage assessment due from Sam Paul		
12	Jan. 4	Security Deposit Liability	500	
		Accounts Receivable		500
		Security deposit withheld for damage		

The first transaction *increases* (debits) accounts receivable and *increases* (credits) other income. You haven't received any money, so why do you increase other income? Because with accrual accounting, you recognize income when you earn it. In this case, you've "earned" $500 (the amount of the damage assesment) even though you haven't received any money.

The second transaction *decreases* (debits) security deposit liability and *decreases* (credits) accounts receivable. As is the case with cash accounting, you decrease security deposit liability when you withhold security; but instead of increasing income, you decrease (credit) accounts receivable. In other words, Sam doesn't owe you $500 anymore because you've taken that amount out of his security deposit.

Next let's look at the bill from Do-It-All General Contracting. Just like before, you record an expense on an accrual basis the moment you owe it.

TRANS. NO.	DATE		DEBIT	CREDIT
13	Jan. 4	Repairs Expense	500	
		Accounts Payable		500
		Bill from Do-It-All General Contracting		

Finally, you write a check to Do-It-All General Contracting after transferring the $500 you withheld to the operating account.

TRANS. NO.	DATE		DEBIT	CREDIT
14	Jan. 4	Operating Bank Account	500	
		Security Deposit Bank Account		500
		Security deposit transfer to operating account		
15	Jan. 5	Accounts Payable	500	
		Operating Bank Account		500
		Payment to Do-It-All General Contracting		

Refunding Security Deposits

After taking care of the damage, you have one last piece of business—refunding the remainder of Sam's deposit. Refunding deposit money is different than withholding it. Instead of increasing (crediting) income, you *decrease* (credit) the cash in your security deposit bank account. In either case, you *decrease* (debit) the security deposit liability on the books.

Let's review what we know:

- You wrote Sam a check for $500 from the security deposit bank account.
- Assets are *debit* accounts; debits *increase* the value of debit accounts.
- Liabilities are *credit* accounts; credits *increase* the value of credit accounts.
- You decreased (credited) the security deposit bank account and decreased (debited) security deposit liability.

YOUR TURN

Go ahead and record the refund in the Arlington's general journal and general ledger

TRANS. NO.	DATE		DEBIT	CREDIT
9	Jan. 4	Operating Bank Account	500	
		Security Deposit Bank Account		500
		Security deposit transfer to operating account		
10	Jan. 5	Repairs Expense	500	
		Operating Bank Account		500
		Payment to Do-It-All General Contracting		
11	Jan. 6	**Security Deposit Liability**		
		Security Deposit Bank Account		
		Security deposit refund to Sam Paul		

Please turn to page 73 of the Appendix to review the complete general ledger and general journal for Chapter 2.

Chapter 3
PROPERTY MANAGER ACCOUNTING

WHILE A PROPERTY manager doesn't necessarily own any property, he is likely overseeing *multiple* properties for different rental owners. So it goes without saying that as important as it is for landlords to keep accurate records, it's even more important for property managers.

With this in mind, it also makes sense that there are many new accounting considerations when it comes to property management. Once again, let's look at the accounting concepts included in this chapter in real world terms. So, for our purposes, you have recently assumed property management duties for Plainville, a four-unit complex owned by an out-of-state rental owner. This means that in addition to keeping the Arlington's books, you are now *also* responsible for keeping a separate set of books for Plainville.

NOTE>>
Keeping accurate records for your rental owners is your legal responsibility in many states. In other words, knowing how to keep accurate books is not only a good idea—it's essential from a legal standpoint.

Setting Up your Company Books and Accounts

As a property manager, you will maintain one set of books for each property *plus* a set of books for your property management company. A major part of keeping your rental owners happy—and, therefore, running a successful business—is keeping their financial records in order.

You now have three sets of books: one for your property management company, one for Arlington, and one for Plainville. As if keeping all of this straight weren't enough, you should also be aware that some transactions will affect the books for both the Plainville *and* your property management company (see page 60 on property management fees for an example). Remember, the key question for consideration throughout this chapter will be which set of books each transaction is recorded in.

In addition to keeping separate books, you will also need to maintain separate bank accounts, each with a distinct purpose. First of all, you'll want to open a bank account for your new property management business. This is where you'll deposit money earned from property management fees. You will also want to open two accounts for the properties you manage. One of these accounts will hold rent income; the other will hold tenant deposits.

Which brings us to your next property management task ...

Collecting Property Reserves

Now that your books and accounts are set up, your next order of business is to collect a property reserve from the out-of-state rental owner. A property reserve is money kept on-hand for unexpected property expenses. For our purposes, the rental owner will provide $500 upfront to cover any unexpected property expenses.

Let's review what we know so far:

- You collected $500 from the rental owner to cover unexpected expenses.
- You deposited the money to the rent bank account; an asset.
- Assets are *debit* accounts; debits *increase* the value of debit accounts.
- The deposit *increased* (debited) the bank balance.
- You need to *credit* another account to offset this debit.

So which account do you credit? The answer is *owner contributions*. Remember that you also used *owner contributions* on page 26 when you set aside $10,000 to fix up the Arlington. You were essentially establishing a property reserve for your property just like Plainville's owner is doing for this property. Therefore, you use owner contributions to record the $500 property reserve for Plainville.

YOUR TURN

Go ahead and record the owner contribution in Plainville's general journal and general ledger.

TRANS. NO.	DATE		DEBIT	CREDIT
1	Dec. 20	Rent Bank Account		
		Owner Contributions		
		Property reserve from rental owner		

ACCRUAL Collecting Property Reserves

Cash accounting readers can skip this section.

Here's how things look on an accrual basis:

TRANS. NO.	DATE		DEBIT	CREDIT
1	Dec. 20	Accounts Receivable	500	
		Owner Contributions		500
		Property reserve due from rental owner		
2	Dec. 20	Rent bank Account	500	
		Accounts Receivable		500
		Property reserve from rental owner		

First you *debit* (increase) accounts receivable $500—the amount you need to collect from the rental owner. Next you *credit* (increase) owner contributions.

Finally, you record the deposit by *debiting* (increasing) the rent bank account and *crediting* (decreasing) accounts receivable.

Giving Rent Concessions

After collecting the property reserve, you turn your attention back to the four-unit complex you're managing. The good news is that three of the four units are rented. The bad news is the one unit that's vacant has been empty for several months. The rental owner tells you he wants $1,000 per month and that he typically requires first and last months' rent and a security deposit upfront. But because the unit has been vacant for so long, he decides to waive the security deposit. As an added incentive, you get him to agree to a $500 rent concession for the first month.

The owner's flexibility pays off. Before long, you find a credit-worthy tenant named Beth Bow. Sensing a good deal, Beth quickly writes you a $500 check for the first month's rent and a $1,000 check for the last, which you then deposit.

So how do you record a rent concession? Think back to how you recorded the $200 rent discount after Sam Paul fixed the steps back on page 40. You credited rent income; but this time instead of debiting repairs, you debit an expense account called *rent concessions*.

YOUR TURN

Go ahead and record the rent concession in Plainville's general journal and general ledger.

TRANS. NO.	DATE		DEBIT	CREDIT
1	Dec. 20	Rent Bank Account	500	
		Owner Contributions		500
		Property reserve from rental owner		
2	Jan. 1	**Rent Concessions Expense**		
		Rent Income		
		Rent concession for first month's rent		

ACCRUAL Giving Rent Concessions

Cash accounting readers can skip this section.

Here's how things look on an accrual basis:

TRANS. NO.	DATE		DEBIT	CREDIT
3	Jan. 1	Rent Concessions Expense	500	
		Accounts Receivable		500
		Rent concession for first month's rent		

First you *debit* (increase) rent concessions $500. Next you *credit* (decrease) accounts receivable. It's as if the rental owner gives Beth $500 (an expense) and Beth then applies it toward the money she owes (accounts receivable).

Collecting Prepaid Rent

Next you need to record Beth's first and last months' rent payments. Because her last month's rent does not yet belong to the rental owner (it won't until the last month of Beth's lease), you're going to deposit that check to your deposit bank account.

Again, let's review what we know:

- You deposited Beth's $500 check to the rent account and her $1,000 check to the deposit account.
- The $500 is rent income and the $1,000 is a prepaid rent liability (because it belongs to Beth until the last month of her lease).
- Assets are *debit* accounts; debits *increase* the value of debit accounts.
- Income and liabilities are *credit* accounts; credits *increase* the value of credit accounts.

YOUR TURN

Go ahead and record Beth's first and last months' rent payments in Plainville's general journal and general ledger.

TRANS. NO.	DATE		DEBIT	CREDIT
2	Jan. 1	Rent Concessions Expense	500	
		Rent Income		500
		Rent concession for first month's rent		
3	Jan. 1	**Rent Bank Account**		
		Rent Income		
		First month's rent from Beth Bow		
4	Jan. 1	**Deposit Bank Account**		
		Prepaid Rent Liability		
		Last month's rent from Beth Bow		

ACCRUAL Collecting Prepaid Rent

Cash accounting readers can skip this section.

Here's how things look on an accrual basis:

TRANS. NO.	DATE		DEBIT	CREDIT
4	Jan. 1	Accounts Receivable	2,000	
		Rent Income		1,000
		Prepaid Rent Liability		1,000
		First and last month's rent due from Beth Bow		
5	Jan. 1	Rent Bank Account	500	
		Accounts Receivable		500
		First month's rent from Beth Bow		
6	Jan. 1	Deposit Bank Account	1,000	
		Accounts Receivable		1,000
		Last month's rent from Beth Bow		

First you *debit* (increase) accounts receivable $2,000—the amount owed for first and last months' rent. Next you record the two payments you deposited by *debiting* (increasing) the rent and deposit bank accounts and *crediting* (decreasing) accounts receivable.

NOTE>>

Management fees are both an expense to your rental owners *and* income to your management company. Because this guide is primarily concerned with keeping the books for the properties you manage, we're going to ignore the entries made on your company's books.

Paying Management Fees

Beth moves in and several days go by. Before you know it, you realize it's time to collect your management fees. You write yourself a $200 check (the amount of your management fee) from the rent bank account and deposit it to your company's operating account.

Let's review what we know:

- You wrote yourself a $200 check for management fees from the rent bank account.
- The bank account is an asset and management fees are an expense.
- Assets and expenses are *debit* accounts; debits *increase* the value of debit accounts.
- The check *decreased* (credited) the bank balance and *increased* (debited) management fees expense.

YOUR TURN

Go ahead and record the expense in Plainville's general journal and general ledger.

TRANS. NO.	DATE		DEBIT	CREDIT
3	Jan. 1	Rent Bank Account	500	
		Rent Income		500
		First month's rent from Beth Bow		
4	Jan. 1	Deposit Bank Account	1,000	
		Prepaid Rent Liability		1,000
		Last month's rent from Beth Bow		
5	Jan. 10	**Management Fees Expense**		
		Rent Bank Account		
		Payment to management company		

ACCRUAL ## Paying Management Fees

Cash accounting readers can skip this section.

Here's how things look on an accrual basis:

TRANS. NO.	DATE		DEBIT	CREDIT
7	Jan. 10	Management Fees Expense	200	
		Accounts Payable		200
		Bill from management company		
8	Jan. 10	Accounts Payable	200	
		Rent Bank Account		200
		Payment to management company		

Paying Rental Owners

After paying yourself, it's time to pay your rental owner. Taking the $500 rent concession and your management fee into account, the Plainville has $800 sitting in the bank. You need to keep $500 of that on-hand for unexpected expenses, so that leaves $300 for the rental owner.

Here's what we know:

- You wrote your rental owner a check for $300 from the rent bank account.
- Bank accounts are asset accounts.
- Asset accounts are *debit* accounts; debits *increase* the value of debit accounts.
- The check *decreased* (credited) the bank balance.

You need to debit another account to offset the credit.

What account do you debit? The answer is an equity account called *owner draws*. An owner draw is an amount an owner takes out of his business (or property) for personal use. Remember credits *increase* the value of equity accounts. In this case, the rental owner is taking money out of the property, so you need to *debit* the account to decrease it.

TRANS. NO.	DATE		DEBIT	CREDIT
5	Jan. 10	Management Fees Expense	200	
		Rent Bank Account		200
		Payment to management company		
6	Jan. 15	**Owner Draws**		
		Rent Bank Account		
		Payment to rental owner		

Collecting Late Fees

A few months go by without incident until Beth misses her rent payment on May 1. Because she has not yet paid by the end of the three-day grace period, you charge a $50 late fee on May 4. Beth apologizes for being late and writes you a check for $1,050 on May 5, which you deposit the same day.

Here's what we know:

- Beth wrote a check for $1,050 on May 5 to cover her rent and the late fee.
- You deposited Beth's check to the rent bank account the same day.
- Rent and late fees are both income.
- Income accounts are *credit* accounts; credits *increase* the value of credit accounts.

YOUR TURN

Go ahead and record Beth's payment in Plainville's general journal and general ledger.

TRANS. TNO.	DATE		DEBIT	CREDIT
6	Jan. 15	Owner Draws	300	
		Rent Bank Account		300
		Payment to rental owner		
7	May 5	**Rent Bank Account**		
		Late Fee Income		
		Rent Income		
		Rent payment from Beth Bow		

ACCRUAL **Collecting Late Fees**

Cash accounting readers can skip this section.

When you do things on an accrual basis, you record $1,000 of income on May 1 and another $50 on May 4, even though Beth has not yet paid either amount.

Here's what we know:

- Beth owes $1,000 for rent on May 1 and an additional $50 late fee on May 4.
- Rent and late fees are both income.
- Credits *increase* the value of income accounts.
- *Accounts receivable* is a special asset account that represents money tenants owe.
- Debits *increase* the value of asset accounts.

TRANS. NO.	DATE		DEBIT	CREDIT
10	May 1	Accounts Receivable	1,000	
		Rent Income		1,000
		May rent due from Beth Bow		
11	May 4	Accounts Receivable	50	
		Late Fee Income		50
		Late fee due from Beth Bow		

On May 1, you debit (increase) accounts receivable $1,000 and credit (increase) rent income. On May 4, you debit accounts receivable another $50 and credit late fee income. At this point, Beth owes $1,050.

Here's what happens when you collect the money and make the deposit on May 5.

TRANS. NO.	DATE		DEBIT	CREDIT
12	May 5	Rent Bank Account	1,050	
		Accounts Receivable		1,050
		Payment from Beth Bow		

You *debit* (increase) the rent bank account and *credit* (decrease) accounts receivable, bringing Beth's accounts receivable balance down to $0.

Refunding an Overpayment

At the end of Beth's lease, she gives notice that she will be vacating her unit. She writes you a check for $1,000, forgetting that she pre-paid her last month's rent when she moved in. Soon after depositing the check, you realize the mistake and write her a check to refund the overpayment.

Let's review what we know:

- You deposited Beth's check for her last month's rent to the rent account.
- You wrote Beth a check for the same amount out of the rent account.
- Credits *increase* income and debits *increase* assets.

YOUR TURN

Go ahead and record Beth's overpayment and refund in Plainville's general journal and general ledger.

TRANS. NO.	DATE		DEBIT	CREDIT
7	May 5	Rent Bank Account	1,050	
		Late Fee Income		50
		Rent Income		1,000
		Rent payment from Beth Bow		
8	Dec. 1	**Rent Bank Account**		
		Rent Income		
		Rent payment from Beth Bow		
9	Dec. 1	**Rent Income**		
		Rent Bank Account		
		Refund to Beth Bow for overpayment		

Applying Prepaid Rent

After refunding Beth's overpayment, you apply Beth's prepaid rent deposit ($1,000) toward her last month's rent and then transfer the amount from the deposit account to the rent account.

So what happens when you apply Beth's prepaid rent deposit to her rent? Remember, you recorded a prepaid rent liability on the books when you collected her money because it still belonged to Beth. When you apply Beth's prepaid rent deposit, you remove the liability *and* recognize rent income equal to the amount applied (similar to the way you recognize income when you withhold a tenant's security deposit).

Here's what we know:

- You applied Beth's prepaid rent deposit toward her last month's rent.
- You transferred $1,000 from the deposit account to the rent account.
- Credits *increase* income and liabilities and debits *increase* assets.

YOUR TURN

Go ahead and record these transactions in Plainville's general journal and general ledger.

TRANS. NO.	DATE		DEBIT	CREDIT
8	Dec. 1	Rent Bank Account	1,000	
		Rent Income		1,000
		Rent payment from Beth Bow		
9	Dec. 1	*Rent Income*	1,000	
		Rent Bank Account		1,000
		Refund to Beth Bow for overpayment		
10	Dec. 1	**Prepaid Rent Liability**		
		Rent Income		
		Prepaid deposit applied to rent		
11	Dec. 1	**Rent Bank Account**		
		Deposit Bank Account		
		Prepaid deposit transfer to rent account		

ACCRUAL ## Applying Prepaid Rent

Cash accounting readers can skip this section.

Here's what happens on an accrual basis:

TRANS. NO.	DATE		DEBIT	CREDIT
15	Dec. 1	Accounts Receivable	1,000	
		Rent Income		1,000
		December rent due from Beth Bow		
16	Dec. 1	Prepaid Rent Liability	1,000	
		Accounts Receivable		1,000
		Prepaid deposit applied to rent		
17	Dec. 1	Rent Rank Account	1,000	
		Deposit Bank Account		1,000
		Prepaid deposit transfer to rent account		

The first transaction *increases* (debits) accounts receivable and *increases* (credits) rent income. The second transaction *decreases* (debits) prepaid rent liability and *decreases* (credits) accounts receivable. As is the case with cash accounting, you decrease prepaid rent liability when you apply it to rent; but instead of increasing income, you decrease (credit) accounts receivable. In other words, Beth doesn't owe you $1,000 for her last month's rent because you collected it upfront when she signed the lease.

> Please turn to page 78 of the Appendix to review the complete general ledger and general journal for Chapter 3.

APPENDIX

Congratulations!

By now you should be able to handle all of the basic property management transactions. Because much of this information is not necessarily intuitive, when you start out you should refer back to this guide whenever necessary. Before long, though, you'll find yourself completing these day-to-day transactions without thinking twice.

In this chapter you'll find the complete general ledgers and general journals from Chapters 2 and 3 to check your work.

If you are interested in learning more about accounting or additional transactions, we recommend *Bookkeeping Made Simple* by David A. Flannery and *The Accounting Game: Basic Accounting Fresh from the Lemonade Stand* by Darrell Mullis and Judith Orloff. For questions about Buildium's online property management software, contact us at sales@buildium.com or visit us at www.buildium.com.

Chapter 2 Cash Basis: Complete General Journal

TRANS. NO.	DATE		DEBIT	CREDIT
1	Dec. 1	Operating Bank Account	10,000	
		Owner Contributions		10,000
		Initial capital investment for the Arlington		
2	Dec. 5	Maintenance Expense	2,000	
		Operating Bank Account		2,000
		Payment to Do-It-All General Contracting		
3	Dec. 6	Advertising Expense	75	
		Business Credit Card		75
		Payment to local newspaper		
4	Dec. 22	Operating Bank Account	2,000	
		Rent Income		1,000
		Security Deposit Liability		1,000
		Security deposit and first month's rent payment from Sam Paul		
5	Dec. 22	Security Deposit Bank Account	1,000	
		Operating Bank Account		1,000
		Security deposit transfer to security deposit account		
6	Apr. 28	Repairs Expense	200	
		Rent Income		200
		Rent adjustment for repairs by Sam Paul		
7	May 1	Operating Bank Account	800	
		Rent Income		800
		Rent payment from Sam Paul		
8	Jan. 4	Security Deposit Liability	500	
		Other Income		500
		Security deposit withheld for damage		
9	Jan. 4	Operating Bank Account	500	
		Security Deposit Bank Account		500
		Security deposit transfer to operating account		
10	Jan. 5	Repairs Expense	500	
		Operating Bank Account		500
		Payment to Do-It-All General Contracting		
11	Jan. 6	Security Deposit Liability	500	
		Security Deposit Bank Account		500
		Security deposit refund to Sam Paul		

Chapter 2 Cash Basis: Complete General Ledger

OPERATING BANK ACCOUNT

TRANS. NO.	DEBIT	CREDIT
1	10,000	
2		2,000
4	2,000	
5		1,000
7	800	
9	500	
10		500

BUSINESS CREDIT CARD

TRANS. NO.	DEBIT	CREDIT
3		75

OWNER CONTRIBUTIONS

TRANS. NO.	DEBIT	CREDIT
1		10,000

SECURITY DEPOSIT BANK ACCOUNT

TRANS. NO.	DEBIT	CREDIT
5	1,000	
9		500
11		500

OTHER INCOME

TRANS. NO.	DEBIT	CREDIT
8		500

MAINTENANCE EXPENSE

TRANS. NO.	DEBIT	CREDIT
2	2,000	

REPAIRS EXPENSE

TRANS. NO.	DEBIT	CREDIT
6	200	
10	500	

RENT INCOME

TRANS. NO.	DEBIT	CREDIT
4		1,000
6		200
7		800

SECURITY DEPOSIT LIABILITY

TRANS. NO.	DEBIT	CREDIT
4		1,000
8	500	
11	500	

ADVERTISING EXPENSE

TRANS. NO.	DEBIT	CREDIT
3	75	

Chapter 2 `ACCRUAL` Complete General Ledger

TRANS. NO.	DATE		DEBIT	CREDIT
1	Dec. 1	Operating Bank Account	10,000	
		Owner Contributions		10,000
		Initial capital investment for the Arlington		
2	Dec. 5	Maintenance Expense	2,000	
		Accounts Payable		2,000
		Bill from Do-It-All General Contracting		
3	Dec. 5	Accounts Payable	2,000	
		Operating Bank Account		2,000
		Payment to Do-It-All General Contracting		
4	Dec. 6	Advertising Expense	75	
		Business Credit Card		75
		Payment to local newspaper		
5	Dec. 22.	Accounts Receivable	2,000	
		Rent Income		1,000
		Security Deposit Liability		1,000
		Security deposit and first month's rent due from Sam Paul		
6	Dec. 22	Operating Bank Account	2,000	
		Accounts Receivable		2,000
		Security deposit and first month's rent payment from Sam Paul		
7	Dec. 22	Security Deposit Bank Account	1,000	
		Operating Bank Account		1,000
		Security deposit transfer to security deposit account		
8	Apr. 28	Repairs Expense	200	
		Accounts Receivable		200
		Rent adjustment for repairs by Sam Paul		
9	May 1	Accounts Receivable	1,000	
		Rent Income		1,000
		Rent due from Sam Paul		
10	May 1	Operating Bank Account	800	
		Accounts Receivable		800
		Rent payment from Sam Paul		
11	Jan. 4	Accounts Receivable	500	
		Other Income		500
		Damage assessment due from Sam Paul		

TRANS. NO.	DATE		DEBIT	CREDIT
12	Jan. 4	Security Deposit Liability	500	
		Accounts Receivable		500
		Security deposit withheld for damage		
13	Jan. 4	Repairs Expense	500	
		Accounts Payable		500
		Bill from Do-It-All General Contracting		
14	Jan. 4	Operating Bank Account	500	
		Security Deposit Bank Account		500
		Security deposit transfer to operating account		
15	Jan. 5	Accounts Payable	500	
		Operating Bank Account		500
		Payment to Do-It-All General Contracting		
16	Jan. 6	Security Deposit Liability	500	
		Security Deposit Bank Account		500
		Security deposit refund to Sam Paul		

OPERATING BANK ACCOUNT

TRANS. NO.	DEBIT	CREDIT
1	10,000	
3		10,000
6	2,000	
7		1,000
10	800	
14	500	
15		500

ACCOUNTS PAYABLE

TRANS. NO.	DEBIT	CREDIT
2		2,000
3	2,000	
13		500
15	500	

ADVERTISING EXPENSE

TRANS. NO.	DEBIT	CREDIT
4	75	

OWNER CONTRIBUTIONS

TRANS. NO.	DEBIT	CREDIT
1		10,000

SECURITY DEPOSIT BANK ACCOUNT

TRANS. NO.	DEBIT	CREDIT
7	1,000	
14		500
16		500

OTHER INCOME

TRANS. NO.	DEBIT	CREDIT
11		500

SECURITY DEPOSIT LIABILITY

TRANS. NO.	DEBIT	CREDIT
5		1,000
12	500	
16	500	

MAINTENANCE EXPENSE

TRANS. NO.	DEBIT	CREDIT
2	2,000	

RENT INCOME

TRANS. NO.	DEBIT	CREDIT
5		1,000
9		1,000

ACCOUNTS RECEIVABLE

TRANS. NO.	DEBIT	CREDIT
5	2,000	
6		2,000
8		200
9	1,000	
10		800
11	500	
12		500

BUSINESS CREDIT CARD

TRANS. NO.	DEBIT	CREDIT
4		75

REPAIRS EXPENSE

TRANS. NO.	DEBIT	CREDIT
8	200	
13	500	

Chapter 3 Cash Basis: Complete General Journal

TRANS. NO.	DATE		DEBIT	CREDIT
1	Dec. 20	Rent Bank Account	500	
		Owner Contributions		500
		Property reserve from rental owner		
2	Jan. 1	Rent Concessions Expense	500	
		Rent Income		500
		Rent concession for first month's rent		
3	Jan. 1	Rent Bank Account	500	
		Rent Income		500
		First month's rent from Beth Bow		
4	Jan. 1	Deposit Bank Account	1,000	
		Prepaid Rent Liability		1,000
		Last month's rent from Beth Bow		
5	Jan. 10	Management Fees Expense	200	
		Rent Bank Account		200
		Payment to management company		
6	Jan. 15	Owner Draws	300	
		Rent Bank Account		300
		Payment to rental owner		
7	May 5	Rent Bank Account	1,050	
		Late Fee Income		50
		Rent Income		1,000
		Rent payment from Beth Bow		
8	Dec. 1	Rent Bank Account	1,000	
		Rent Income		1,000
		Rent payment from Beth Bow		
9	Dec. 1	Rent Income	1,000	
		Rent Bank Account		1,000
		Refund to Beth Bow for overpayment		
10	Dec. 1	Prepaid Rent Liability	1,000	
		Rent Income		1,000
		Prepaid deposit applied to rent		
11	Dec. 1	Rent Bank Account	1,000	
		Deposit Bank Account		1,000
		Prepaid deposit transfer to rent account		

Chapter 3 Cash Basis: Complete General Ledger

RENT BANK ACCOUNT

TRANS. NO.	DEBIT	CREDIT
1	500	
3	500	
5		200
6		300
7	1,050	
8	1,000	
9		1,000
11	1,000	

MANAGEMENT FEES EXPENSE

TRANS. NO.	DEBIT	CREDIT
5	200	

RENT INCOME

TRANS. NO.	DEBIT	CREDIT
2		500
3		500
7		1,000
8		1,000
9	1,000	
10		1,000

RENT CONCESSIONS EXPENSE

TRANS. NO.	DEBIT	CREDIT
2	200	

OWNER DRAWS

TRANS. NO.	DEBIT	CREDIT
6	300	

DEPOSIT BANK ACCOUNT

TRANS. NO.	DEBIT	CREDIT
4	1,000	
11		1,000

LATE FEE INCOME

TRANS. NO.	DEBIT	CREDIT
7		50

PREPAID RENT LIABILITY

TRANS. NO.	DEBIT	CREDIT
4		1,000
10	1,000	

OWNER CONTRIBUTIONS

TRANS. NO.	DEBIT	CREDIT
1		500

Chapter 3 ![ACCRUAL] Complete General Journal

TRANS. NO.	DATE		DEBIT	CREDIT
1	Dec. 20	Accounts Receivable	500	
		Owner Contributions		500
		Property reserve due from rental owner		
2	Dec. 20	Rent Bank Account	500	
		Accounts Receivable		500
		Property reserve from rental owner		
3	Jan. 1	Rent Concessions Expense	500	
		Accounts Receivable		500
		Rent concession for first month's rent		
4	Jan. 1	Accounts Receivable	2,000	
		Rent Income		1,000
		Prepaid Rent Liability		1,000
		First and last month's rent *due from Beth Bow*		
5	Jan. 1	Rent Bank Account	500	
		Accounts Receivable		500
		First month's rent from Beth Bow		
6	Jan. 1	Deposit Bank Account	1,000	
		Accounts Receivable		1,000
		Last month's rent from Beth Bow		
7	Jan. 10	Management Fees Expense	200	
		Accounts Payable		200
		Bill from management company		
8	Jan. 10	Accounts Payable	200	
		Rent Bank Account		200
		Payment to management company		
9	Jan. 15	Owner Draws	300	
		Rent Bank Account		300
		Payment to rental owner		
10	May 1	Accounts Receivable	1,000	
		Rent Income		1,000
		May rent due from Beth Bow		
11	May 4	Accounts Receivable	50	
		Late Fee Income		50
		Late fee due from Beth Bow		
12	May 5	Rent Bank Account	1,050	
		Accounts Receivable		1,050
		Rent payment from Beth Bow		

TRANS. NO.	DATE		DEBIT	CREDIT
13	Dec. 1	Rent Bank Account	1,000	
		Rent Income		1,000
		Rent payment from Beth Bow		
14	Dec. 1	Rent Income	1,000	
		Rent Bank Account		1,000
		Refund to Beth Bow for overpayment		
15	Dec. 1	Accounts Receivable	1,000	
		Rent Income		1,000
		December rent due from Beth Bow		
16	Dec. 1	Prepaid Rent Liability	1,000	
		Accounts Receivable		1,000
		Prepaid deposit applied to rent		
17	Dec. 1	Rent Bank Account	1,000	
		Deposit Bank Account		1,000
		Prepaid deposit transfer to rent account		

RENT BANK ACCOUNT

TRANS. NO.	DEBIT	CREDIT
2	500	
5	500	
8		200
9		300
12	1,050	
13	1,000	
14		1,000
17	1,000	

BUSINESS CREDIT CARD

TRANS. NO.	DEBIT	CREDIT
4		75

RENT CONCESSIONS EXPENSE

TRANS. NO.	DEBIT	CREDIT
3	500	

OWNER DRAWS

TRANS. NO.	DEBIT	CREDIT
9	300	

ACCOUNTS RECEIVABLE

TRANS. NO.	DEBIT	CREDIT
1	500	
2		500
3		500
4	2,000	
5		500
6		1,000
10	1,000	
11	50	
12		1,050
15	1,000	
16		1,000

MANAGEMENT FEES EXPENSE

TRANS. NO.	DEBIT	CREDIT
7	200	

OWNER CONTRIBUTIONS

TRANS. NO.	DEBIT	CREDIT
1		500

DEPOSIT BANK ACCOUNT

TRANS. NO.	DEBIT	CREDIT
6	1,000	
17		1,000

LATE FEE INCOME

TRANS. NO.	DEBIT	CREDIT
11		50

RENT INCOME

TRANS. NO.	DEBIT	CREDIT
4		1,000
10		1,000
13		1,000
14	1,000	
15		1,000

PREPAID RENT LIABILITY

TRANS. NO.	DEBIT	CREDIT
4		1,000
16	1,000	

Made in the USA
Middletown, DE
09 January 2022